A Dream Is a Wish The Heart Makes

OR if at first you don't succeed, Change the rules.

By: Grace Allison

This book is a work of fiction. Places, events, and situations in this story are purely fictional. Any resemblance to actual persons, living or dead, is coincidental.

© 2004 by Grace Allison. All rights reserved.

No part of this book may be reproduced, stored in a retrieval system, or transmitted by any means, electronic, mechanical, photocopying, recording or otherwise, without written permission from the author.

ISBN: 9780692486122 (Paperback)

Library of Congress Control Number: 2004090310

This book is printed on acid free paper.

Printed in the United States of America

Dedicated to

All people

Seeking wholeness,

Loving and peace

Gratitude

This book would not exist if I had not discovered
the sacred inner awareness of my soul through
The Beloved Jesus Christ
The loving teachings of John-Roger and
The Movement of Spiritual Inner Awareness

Special thanks to my many mentors including
George Koch, Ernie Hill and Vito Rigello who encouraged my
creativity

Thanks to author and writing coach Jeff Davis
who patiently supported me to write and follow my dream

Thank you my beloved loving friend and soul mate John Ball
for your wisdom and loving care

Thank you Laren Bright for your years of friendship and
contributions to this work

Thank you Sandi DeVeau for your loving friendship
and support of my writing and creativity

Thanks to some of the first participants of the early workshops
who inspired this work,
Sandi DeVeau, Linda Motweiller, Moreah Fritz, Barbara Martin,
Elisa Pardo

Contents

Testimonial VII

Can You Handle Happiness? IX

How To Read This Book XI

Preface............................. XII

Introduction XIV

PART ONE - CONCEPTS............... XVII

1 At First You Don't Succeed, Change The Rules. XVIII

2 Who Will Rescue Me? XXI

3 Spiritual Poverty XXV

4 In The Beginning There Was God XXXII

PART TWO - WORKBOOK XL

5 Keys To Creating Greater Freedom Within 1

6 Blessed Are The Poor In Spirit............... 4

7 The Value Of Prayer......................19

8 Image I Am A God Energized Be-Ing 25

9 Keys Of Awareness 33

10 Creating Your Dream................... 38

Testimonial

After the death of my husband two years ago, I was on a continual search for recreating myself. It seemed that the path I was on had led me to a place that I never wanted to be ... alone without the love of my life. Then I resigned my career position to develop my own consulting company, but along the way I was mugged and all my Identity stolen ... twice no less. Next was six months of total focus on nothing but repairing all the chaos that a theft ring created. My new career was Identity Theft.

Grace Allison, her book, **A Dream Is A Wish The Heart Makes**, manual and workshop were the perfect vehicle in assisting me to honor what was and embrace what would come. Through this beautiful process that she has so carefully prepared, I found peace ... was released to enter in to a new future filled with possibilities.

Truly, I emerged from the darkness into the Light. Immediately my life changed. No more fear, no more 'wandering in the desert' ... my life had focus, joy and I was empowered to move on. With lightening speed the chaos stopped ... I let go of the grief ... love presented itself again in the form of an amazing man who was drawn to my spirit ... to the Joy, Laughter, Enthusiasm and Energy. I was not 'looking' for love yet it came to me. I attracted this gift because the 'blocks' in my spirit were gone. To experience love so deeply in a Lifetime is a treasured gift. To experience it twice is nothing short of Awesome and quite Humbling. I am at Peace. I AM.

A Dream Is A Wish The Heart Makes is a continuing process ... a joyful adventure that I apply and work daily. Sandi deVeau

Can you Handle More Happiness?

What if you had the ability to be happy more of the time? Would you do it? If you would, here's the book that will tell you how.

In clear, direct, everyday language, A Dream is A Wish The Heart Makes describes how life's challenges can distract us from our happiness and provides do-able techniques for redirecting ourselves back to our natural joy and fulfillment.

Our world is in a process of change, and change is one of the key elements to most peoples' discomfort and distraction from their happiness. Yet change doesn't have to be difficult. In this book you will find keys to:

- Understand change
- Re-define change so it doesn't have to be distressing
- Use situations of change to propel you forward
- Empower yourself no matter what life throws at you

Though the techniques presented here appear simple, they are powerful and can produce profound results. They are in the language of today, yet many are secrets once known only by ancient mystics. Their effectiveness for you is limited only by your willingness to work them.

If you are ready for more happiness, this book will put you on the fast track to having it.

Grace Allison is a successful wellness, business development and marketing coach. She has faced many life challenges, including a life-threatening disease, and used what she encountered as a stimulus to gain greater happiness and fulfillment. She lives in Dallas, Texas, where she leads workshops and maintains a private health and success coaching practice.

How To Read This Book

In "Part One" of "A Dream Is A Wish The Heart Makes", I will introduce some new concepts to you.

In "Part Two", is a workbook that you will use to change your life and create your dream.

Grace Allison, Author

Preface

Out of the Darkness Comes the Light

I have a soulful purpose in writing this book that offers people wisdom, perspective and practical guidance. It is my desire that the book's reflective areas will speak directly to your heart. The Biblical background is given in expository areas to provide information to assist you perhaps in perspective to your own situations. Perhaps you will see your own personal problems and needs in the context of the broader human context. The exercises in this book have the potential to guide you through dealing with your own situations and changing your life and redirecting your energy.

Our planet is returning to a time and place of sacredness, once known as the Garden of Eden. God is calling us to trust our creative inner spirit and inner knower. Through serving the greater good in each other, and ourselves we are reaching past our fears and becoming a community of people who experience more peace with greater health, wealth, happiness, abundance, prosperity and riches. A place we all remember and are trying to find again.

The time is now! Are you in a place in your life where you are just tired of being tired, of being sick, of being sick and tired? Are you ready to learn how to live in the present? Are you willing to stand on your own two feet and respond to your life with wisdom, discernment, love, courage, determination and strength? Do you want to live in your own Garden of Eden? Do you want to create freedom from within?

Introduction

Change

Do You Like It? No, you probably don't. Since World War II, our society has been affected by drastic change through forces of fear. Corporate downsizing, Y2K, road rage, mass murders, and acts of terrorism. Fear is a destructive force and a cultural phenomenon. All fears, no matter what they are, separate us from ourselves. Fear closes down our creative imagination. By imagination, I mean our social contact and communication with one another. The long-term effects of living in constant fear are isolation as well as mental and physical deterioration, a numb-ing of the spirit. It can destroy people and their lives only *if* they allow it.

As a child, I lived in constant fear. My father, an abusive alcoholic, raged most of the time. My mother, in and out of mental institutions most of her life, eventually committed suicide. My siblings and I felt like prisoners in a concentration camp. Powerless and humiliated, we lived daily in fear.

Being a victim, I learned helplessness. I felt I no longer had choices in my life. I became passive and someone who would do anything to please. As I grew up, the **shame** of who I was became deeper and deeper with each mental, emotional and physical blow. Fear was all I knew. At ten years old my parents gave me the job of raising my five brothers and sisters. I had no social life or friends. I had no boundaries and no protection. I only had hope that someone would rescue me.

I was so covered with shame and fear that I did not know who I really was. I ran away from home at 16, only to marry a man who was equally as controlling as my father. At age 30, after two marriages, I was physically, mentally, emotionally and spiritually bankrupt. I recognized that although each marriage was about 10 years apart, with different people, they were similar. Fear was robbing me of my soul. Shame made me feel unworthy to love and be loved in a healthy way. I had no identity. I knew I had to change. Healing my feelings of shame and redirecting my fears became my life's work. I had to stop doing whatever I was doing and change.

Part One

Concepts

CHAPTER 1

If at First You Don't Succeed,

Change the Rules

I recognized that my behavior was not getting me where I wanted to be. I wanted to feel love and be loved, unconditionally, to be able to be vulnerable, safe and intimate. I had a strong will and thought I could control and respond to fear by controlling my outer environment of people and things. It only made my life crazier. The energy it took to keep all that going just became too much to keep up. One day I just couldn't do it anymore. I wanted to relax, be happy. That was the day I lost my mind and found my heart.

Low self-esteem had developed over the years of feeling unworthy. How could I have a life of **goodness**? The two were mutually exclusive. I had an inspired question. How could I use my inner energy of thoughts and feelings differently?

With some caring counselors and ministers, I began to learn about trust. I found inside myself a spiritual knowing. A Higher Power, the inner Light of God was beginning to awaken inside of me. Everything inside of me and outside of me was connected to a consciousness that had insight and knowledge more powerful than I could ever imagine. I became a spiritual scientist. By using my life experiences as a life lab of learning and growing, my life assumed new dimensions. I studied the Quantum Theory of energy. I discovered that mind and matter are forms of energy. I learned that energy follows thought, and what you imagine and feel can create your reality. I learned through my creative imagination and prayer to give up control. I started by letting go and allowing God and the Holy Spirit within me to heal my deep mental and emotional wounds. To create a new path, I had to say, "Yes" to life, not "No".

Fear is challenging each person to awaken to his or her loving inside. Some of us are being tested with lost jobs, and dying family members, or perhaps like me, you've had toxic family issues and serious illness or maybe your home may have been destroyed in a natural disaster. These challenges are all part of the greater change that God is delivering to each person. It is a time of reassessment and inner discovery. Change can be scary, but it doesn't have to be. God is calling us to be more accountable in our relationship with each other and ourselves. We have **opportunities and choices** to make. Will we respond to our opportunities with love or with fear?

Through my life lessons and God's creative inner spirit, I have created the following process I call, "A Dream Is A Wish The Heart Makes". It is a process that aligns and strengthens the inner spirit with your outer life. Through this process you can learn how to shift your inner resources from feeling out of control to experiencing inner freedom, inner strength, peace, confidence and love.

CHAPTER 2

Who Will Rescue Me?

The song "Rescue Me", from the 1960's is about a young woman who wanted to have a man take her into his arms and make her life happy by filling her every need and desire. I was about 15 at the time that song came out. By that time, with no self-esteem, I needed a man to take care of me. I was following the rigid sex roles of our society. I wanted to be perfect and have the perfect life. I was taught that men, strong and decisive never show weakness, emotions or vulnerability. Women, the helpmates of real men are the caretakers of the home and family. Emotional, vulnerable and fragile they are the peacemakers, often making peace at any price. I was seeking "romantic love." I was looking for a prince to come and reward me for all I was giving up, the reward being that my prince would take care of me for the rest of my life.

In the newspaper the other day, the first cell of a cartoon read, "you will, from now on, not have one single thought that is your own." The next cell in the cartoon was a man and woman standing in front of a minister as the woman said, "I do." The message behind the song and the cartoon is based on the ancient myth that men are supposed to be in charge of every thought and emotion that women have and fulfill their every need. The knight in shining armour would rescue the princess.

Many people still believe this myth. Where in the world or world history (at least in western civilization) did these cultural roles develop? How have we become a society of needy dependency? Patriarchal societies emerged thousands of years ago. For instance, in Greece, 500 BCE (at least), women clearly were men's property.

St. Augustine, one of the great fathers of the Catholic Church is well known for his view of women. "What is the difference," he wrote to a friend, "whether it is in a wife or mother, it is still Eve the temptress that we must beware of in any woman." Woman's only function was the child bearing which passed the contagion of Original Sin to the next generation, like a venereal disease. Western Christianity never fully recovered.

During the middle ages the church provided an all-encompassing context for people's lives. From birth to death the church interwove fear-filled messages. People lived in submission to the words of the priests, who were deemed mediator between God and man.

The old religions that embraced the connection to the natural world were destroyed. We lost our connection to creation. We banished the intuitive, pattern-perceiving parts of our selves. The feminine, receptive, holistic way of seeing had been replaced with a blind faith in the truncated rational mind – a mind that understands force and not flow, either/or instead of both. Competition instead of cooperation, power over instead of power with, short-term thinking instead of planning for the future of our grandchildren.

Over the ages we have turned against our intuition and grown to mistrust its symbols, devaluing our creativity. It is the experience of soul we hunger for. Dreams, stories, and myths have been relegated to make-believe. They are not honored for their healing and prophetic qualities that have guided human beings through the ages. The mistrust of the imagination is a result of mystical experience being confused with superstition and magical thinking, which is hidden in the shadow of the church.

One of the biggest obstacles of growth is our view of God. The first aspect of that shift has to be the shift from a God of law to a God of grace. People must discover that God is **for** them and not **against** them. This is what it means to have a God of Grace and a God of mercy. Jesus had a mission to show people what God was really like. "Immanuel", one of the names given to Jesus, means, "God with us." And when Jesus walked the earth, he showed us a very different God than we might expect. The kingdom of heaven is within each person; **everyone,** not just the priests and ministers, has access to His divine guidance.

CHAPTER 3

Spiritual Poverty

The need to be rescued is a cultural phenomenon that affects many areas of our society today. We are in a severe state of neediness and incompleteness that has rendered us spiritually impoverished. Not everyone is aware of his or her neediness. Jesus described those who are aware of their neediness *as poor in spirit*. The Greek word for "poor in spirit" is *ptochos* which means a cringing beggar, absolutely dependent on others for survival. Jesus said, "Blessed are the poor in spirit, for theirs is the kingdom of heaven." (Matthew 5:3). Our state of incompleteness drives us outside of ourselves to God as the source of healing and hope.

Broken heartedness is related to spiritual poverty. It is the state of being wounded or crushed by some loss, person, hurt, injustice or circumstance. When a person is downcast because of an emotional, relational, or career injury, he can be brokenhearted. God has a special tenderness for this condition. Broken heartedness often brings about a sense of spiritual poverty as it shows us our need. This dark night of the soul of deep need stems from experiences of feeling unworthy, shameful or guilty. It can feel like a cold blistery wind blowing inside. Who or what will rescue me from my pain? What will fill this empty cold, darkness? To feel so tortured can be like living in hell. What will cover and soothe my inner pain? Some people will eat; others will drink alcohol or use drugs. Some escape with risky sexual behavior, credit cards, gambling and spending money beyond their means or working long hours without a day off or holiday. All of these addictive fear based behaviors are choices based on our inner lack and the want to be rescued.

Spiritual poverty is a rich part of the growth process. The more broken we are the more God can grow us up.

What do we need to be happy and well adjusted? The basic need for any one is food, shelter, air and love. Even having those things, most people still feel need or lack. You may covet many things, particularly material objects and experiences (a car, boat, a stereo, money, sex or maybe chocolate ice cream). Have you noticed when you first acquire or experience them that you may feel great and satisfied; but then, you distance yourself from that thing and go looking for something else to fill the lack or need? Have you ever gone to the grocery store when you were hungry? Did you buy things that you didn't really need because your hunger made those things look good? Ever go out to pick up a person when you were lonely or needy inside, or go shopping at the mall with your credit cards when you felt lonely or sad? There is a difference in taking care of our basic needs and the need we feel from the deep lack of emotional fullness or emptiness.

The need to be rescued by someone or something outside of our self is responsible for co-dependent addictive and often abusive relationships, as well as for financial and health problems. A constant need creates difficulty in all aspects of our life. For example, imagine you have a job but you need money. You're feeling really scared. The job you have isn't the one you really want, but it pays the bills. Maybe you think having money will really make you feel more secure about yourself. In your mind you rationalize (rationing lies) how great you are going to feel and what you are going to get from the situation.

Have you ever heard the statement, "As a man thinketh in his heart he becomes"? What we focus on and put energy into is what we get.

This, is a true story. I knew a man I will call him Eric who thought he could have everything and anything he wanted. He had a great job, a beautiful family and home. He was a manager of a department in a major department store. Eric and a group of his buddies in the store where he worked rationalized (rationing lies) they were not getting paid what they thought they should. One day through a coordinated group effort they decided to take from the store items they wanted but really couldn't afford. After all, they worked long hours, the company owed it to them. Huge delivery trucks loaded with merchandise would show up at each person's home with stolen goods. In addition to stealing from his work, Eric also broke into his own car and filed a claim with his insurance company for money he needed to buy the boat he wanted. Eric's insatiable need for money led him to abuse and cheat on his wife. His escapades lasted about five years. He was in one scheme after another. After a few years his wife felt unsafe with him and could not trust him because of his abuse, stealing and infidelity. What would happen to her if he got caught in any of his schemes? He would not listen. As afraid of him as she was, she divorced him. Within one year after the divorce, he filed bankruptcy. Eric lost everything - the house, the car, boat and all the merchandise he stole from his employer. Because of a slow economy Eric was laid off. The need was a big dark hole inside of him draining him of everything. Trying to get anything from a need is like pushing a rock up a hill. The task becomes near impossible. Finally, when you reach the top, usually it is still not enough. NEED is all you will get. The things you imagine you need are often taken away because of the deep unworthiness and low self-esteem to have and own them. Maybe deep down Eric didn't believe he deserved to have his job, his wife, his home or any of the things he stole.

As a wellness consultant, I have had many people come to me to help them feel better. It is normal for someone who is out of balance physically to be rescued temporarily until they can take care of themselves; however, some of the people I have seen have had more than ten health care practitioners. Somehow they feel "a natural approach" could work better. I ask them what they think I can do that the other ten caregivers were not able to. Most of them have said, "I want to feel happy." One woman I talked with told me she had worked with over 15 different practitioners for over 21 years to "get her son to have a happy life." She had been to doctors, psychiatrists, and natural healers of all kinds. She was a nurse and thought because of her training, she could make her son well, the way *she* wanted him to be. After about two hours of hearing the history of her son's medical past, I asked her, "What does your son want?" She said, "Well, he only wants to sit around the house and stare". Then I asked, "Who does he think is going to rescue him from his life?" The answer was, "According to my son, our minister is going to save him because he claims to be over taken by demons." She thought that vitamin supplements could make him change, make him feel happy and give him the life she wanted him to have. I quietly explained that supplements would not make her son's life much different. All supplements can do is manipulate his natural energy. Natural healing methods cannot change a whole personality. I said, "**Your *son*** has to make the decision to *want* to have a better life. It must be ***his*** intention to use the new energy he feels and imagine a new life where he can *have* something more in his life. You cannot make him change nor can anyone else." I suggested she see a psychologist who specialized in working with this type of behavior.

Healthcare providers like doctors, nurses, firemen, and emergency care people are here to rescue us, but only for a short term until we can get past the injury so we can go on with our lives. Ministers and priests are here to assist us in our lives as counselors. Mothers, fathers and family members are to show their love and wisdom. No one can make another person feel or change. There is no perfect life. We are just being human. So, *who's* really in charge of us?

CHAPTER 4

In The Beginning There Was God

And God created the heavens and the earth. Everything starts out with God as the Source. This is point number one in the Bible. Nothing is creation before God, and everything that exists came from Him. This includes all the "stuff" of life - the resources, the principles, the purposes, the meaning – everything!

After making the "stuff", God made humankind and breathed life into them (Genesis 2:7). We have to understand this means to receive of the Holy Spirit into the troubled areas of our lives. God is not only Creator but also re-creator of life. It becomes the system of how one overcomes a depression or heals a marriage or rescues a failing business career.

God's role is to provide and our role is to receive. Our role is to be a dependent one. Independence is not an option for us. God existed without us, not vice versa. God's role is to be in control; our role is to surrender to God's control of the world and we are to control our self.

It's difficult for some of us to imagine how God's creative energy works inside our mind, heart and subconscious. To do so, imagine Eden. Eden was a sacred place. The experience of living in the garden was peace, reverence, joy, serenity, bliss and love.

I am going to use the story of the Garden of Eden as a metaphor for you to picture how God's creative energy works inside our mind, heart and subconscious.

The Garden of Eden is like ten acres of land all around us. Each person has an energy field (God's vibration) around him or her called an aura it's an invisible atmosphere supposedly surrounding a person or thing. We all have this energy field in and around us. Remember being in an elevator and feeling the person next to you, but you really didn't touch him? This aura of invisible light is what I call our "ten acres" of energy. We are holy temples of God's loving light or energy. We must honor and take care of our personal ten acres. We stand on our own ground *aware* of God's light within us. Eden can be a pleasant, harmonious, productive state of consciousness in which reside all possibilities of growth. When we are expressing in harmony, and bringing forth the qualities of God's grace in divine order, we experience being in Eden, or in a state of bliss in a harmonious body. The "garden" symbolizes the spiritual body in which man dwells when he brings forth his thoughts after the original divine ideas. This garden is the substance of God or state of perfect relation of ideas to Being. With this oneness, we can move forward in our life, with all good things coming to us. In this way, the world is not to be conquered with force and power; it is to be received, with inner strength, wisdom, discernment and love.

In the Garden of Eden God created humans and he put them into relationship, first with Him and then with each other. God made people for Himself and for one another. Adam depended on a relationship with God for life. But even with that relationship, he needed human connection as well. God said, "It is not good to for man to be alone" (Genesis 2:18) Man was incomplete with God alone. Relationships were at the core of the way things were created and there was an order to them.

God placed Adam and Eve in the Garden. Metaphorically, Adam represents our mind and Eve our heart and the snake how we attempt to control our lives by separating from God.

Adam represents the masculine side of our consciousness, our mind. He is the generic man, or the whole human race epitomized in an individual-man idea. The mind has an expression of will, which when combined with God's will creates truth and wisdom. When we are using our mind in a positive expression with wisdom, the energy level inside of us goes up. The negative side of the masculine energy is outward force, power, control and manipulation. Trying to control, manipulate with force is the negative expression of Adam. When we align the mind with wisdom, the mind lets go and is open to receive its balance, Eve.

Eve, the feminine counterpart, represents the heart and is grace, love, or intuitive feeling, in individual consciousness. Woman symbolizes the soul region of man and is the mother principle of God in expression. Eve (feeling) becomes the "mother of all living." Intuitive feeling is spiritual creativity that allows us to receive from deep within our heart. The feeling we experience is love. We are expanding inside creating compassion and empathy. When we are expressing our positive spiritual creativity, our energy levels go up. The negative side of the feminine energy is the seven deadly sins, greed, avarice, gluttony, lust, envy, jealousy and sloth. When we express these energy traits, we feel darkness lackluster and lethargy.

When we combine Adam and Eve, the masculine and feminine energy in our human bodies, we attain the qualities of giving (Adam) and receiving (Eve). Everyone on our planet earth has both masculine and feminine energy. Some people have more masculine energy traits and some more feminine energy traits. The brain (Adam) communicates the will with wisdom to the heart, (Eve). The heart (Eve), in turn, opens by receiving wisdom through grace, intuition and creative insight. The energy of our heart when expressing positive energy with compassion and empathy ascends upward to the mind combined with God's truth and wisdom. At this point we can match our thoughts with our feelings and move on our creative idea to take action in the world receiving all good (God) things.

When Adam and Eve were in the Garden, they had both grace and truth united in one with God. When the snake appeared and tempted them they lost grace and a "truth-full" relationship with God. The snake represents the separation from God as we try to control our environment by using either our mind (negative Adam traits) and/or heart (negative Eve traits). The head of the snake represents projecting our thoughts on the future and really dwelling on "what if's". When we separate our self from God, we are in our mind creating fear as we attempt to control the future. To feel in control, we play lots of games with ourselves and other people through interactions of manipulating situations and trying to control the outcome.

Without grace, Adam and Eve felt shame: when they heard God walking in the garden in the cool of the day, they hid from him. When God called out, "Where are you?" Adam explains that he was hiding because he was afraid (Genesis 3:8-10). Shame and guilt had entered the world; human beings were no longer safe.

When we separate ourselves from our wisdom and truth, our mind and emotions can feel like they are on a roller coaster, with our bodies just trying to keep up. Grace disappears, and emotional pain becomes our suffering. In suffering, the feelings of love and pain often become one and the same. Through addictive behaviors we become adrenaline junkies. We push our bodies to make more and more energy.

Remember Eric and his need for money? Eric's need was based on addictive patterns of lack and low self-esteem. The job he had was un-satisfying. Yet he held onto it because of his need to pay his bills. Through his fear and low self-esteem he created more and more situations that eventually caught up with him. In his heart Eric was not worthy. He was trying to be the perfect man in our society. Make money so he could have all the things that money could buy. He had lack inside which kept him from the Source of all creation, which is God. He thought he could make his life up the way he wanted it. However, he learned an important lesson. He could not control the world around him. He learned that what he put out was a mental and emotional need and what he got back was need.

God is in control of everything inside and outside of us. God's energy is all around us. Eric learned that his job was to surrender his fear and need for control. Like a bad movie, he was creating his life through the illusion of lack. When we are creating negative pictures, either through constantly projecting into the future (anxiety), or revisiting an event in the past (regret), we will continue to create a negative reality. We become spiritually bankrupt, our life becomes one of "getting from someone or something" to fill our lack or need. We seek to find and fill it "out there". In an attempt to get more energy to fill ourselves, we participate in addictive feelings of anger, worry, grief, fear and depression. When a person is continuously stressed by emotional pain, there are subtle changes in the body that create a dependency on stress-related chemistry. Changing habitual patterns of pain can be as difficult as giving up an addictive substance such as nicotine, alcohol or even heroin.

Part Two

Workbook

Chapter 5

Keys to Creating Greater Freedom Within

Introduction

Do you have a dream in your heart that you just can't see how to make come true? If you are truly soul searching for an easier way to live, it begins with awareness of how you are directing your mind and emotion and letting go of the poverty of your spirit, the fear that blocks the loving that is present in your heart.

In Psalm 139:23-24 David asked God to reveal who he was at a deep level: "Search me, O God, and know my heart; test me and know my anxious thoughts. See if there is any offensive way in me, and lead me in the way everlasting. Pray David's prayer along with him, and God will reveal the true state of being in your heart. Ask God to unravel the problems in your ways of attachment. As David says in Psalm 51:6, "Surely you desire truth in the inner parts; you teach me wisdom in the inmost place."

Right now I want you to begin to see your life as classroom. Each day there are life lessons to learn and grow. When life becomes a classroom, the manual you read comes through the wisdom of the heart and intuitive knowing. The skill to hear intuitively is developed by learning how to discipline your body, mind and emotions. The results are more joy and creativity to do and be just about anything you can imagine.

Through "A Dream Is A Wish The Heart Makes" book, manual and workshop you will find thought provoking lessons to assist you in your own life classroom and your personal situations. In the workshop manual at the end of each chapter will be opportunities to explore your inner world through a series of processes that are designed to shift your inner perspective and redirect your inner resources. The intention during these processes is to be really gentle and loving to yourself. I suggest you begin exploring with a childlike curiosity and see where the adventure takes you. Follow through on the processes for at least 30 days. See what happens.

A Dream Is a Wish The Heart Makes

In the workbook you will

__Take an inventory of your current priorities.

__Learn how to create healthy personal boundaries.

__Explore asking for what you want while creating realistic and achievable goals.

__Last, you will learn how to work through the resistance of the internal conditioned patterns that could either be the blocks or stepping stones for you to have what you want easily, pleasurably, safely with fun, joy and enthusiasm.

Let the adventure begin!

Chapter 6

Blessed Are The Poor In Spirit

Mother Teresa defines poverty as the "least of my brethren", as the hungry and the lonely, not only for food but for the Word of God; the thirsty and the ignorant, not only for water but also for knowledge, peace, truth, justice, and love; the naked and unloved, not only for clothes but also for human dignity; the unwanted, the unborn child; the racially discriminated against; the homeless and abandoned, not only for a shelter made of bricks, but for a heart that understands, that covers, that loves the sick, the dying destitute, and the captives, not only in body but also in mind and spirit; all those who have lost all hope

A Dream Is a Wish The Heart Makes

...d faith in life, the alcoholics and drug addicts and all those who have ...st God and who have lost all hope in the power of the Spirit."

...1989, God was giving me a wake-up call; I was diagnosed with ...ervical cancer. Angry and scared, I said to myself, "I can't have cancer I ...ave work to do." I was a fearless competitor pushing my way through ...hatever got in my way. I worked at a pretty intense pace and loved the ...eling of power as I moved effortlessly at high speeds. I had to have ...ealth, possessions and power. I was worshiping the god that all of our ...ociety bows to, *money* and all it can buy. To succeed one must have ...ealth. At all costs one must have wealth.

...had no idea how addicted I had become to **fear**. My broken ...eartedness had created many different faces of fear and worry. Fear of ...ilure, fear of loneliness, fear of intimacy, fear of risk, fear of pain, fear ...f abandonment, fear of rejection, fear of looking or sounding stupid, ...ar of what someone else might think, fear of punishment, fear of ...overty, fear of exploitation and fear of missing the big chance. Fear was ...ke a drug. The more I pushed the better the high. With the ...nnouncement of "cancer", it was *time* to do some serious evaluating. ...ow in the world did I get, *cancer?*

...s much as I thought I was in control of my life, I wasn't. Outwardly I ...ept up appearances of success, nice home, fancy car, credit cards living ...e high life, but inside I was afraid. I was defenseless, neither power nor money could spare me from the empty, lonely darkness I felt inside. I could no longer run away and cover up my broken heart.

I didn't pay attention that I was tired most of the time. Some days I could hardly get out of bed. I blamed my nervousness and anxiety on other people. Every once in a while I would get really angry and blow up at somebody for no real reason. I was having trouble making decisions; my mistakes at work were beginning to show. I was in big trouble. No wonder my immune system shut down. My body was saying, "we are not doing this anymore."

My body went through tremendous changes after the surgery. I lost my high-pressure drive and with it, my job. I cried out what am I going to do now? Who would rescue me? I was alone, afraid to let go of control. I was depressed and struggled for about two years with no real physical energy. It took me losing my mind to find what was really important, my heart. I was feeding my body but starving my soul. I had to change my *attitude*.

With the threat of cancer in my life I was blessed with the opportunity to examine and study my negative beliefs. I did not realize how many negative destructive beliefs I had that were taking the very life out of me. I began to take responsibility and came to understand that whatever I thought and held onto my conscious mind would become real in my body and environment. The thoughts themselves are but mental forms, but when I put feeling into them they became real. I was actually breathing life into every fear, anxiety and worry. My fears hungered for more attention with every breath I took.

It was my dark night of the soul that revealed to me that what I was doing was not working. What could I do to feel good about my life and myself? I remembered hearing a phrase from Jesus Christ when he spoke The Sermon On The Mount. "Take no thought (or be not anxious) saying, what shall we eat, or what shall we drink, or wherewithal shall we be clothed; for your heavenly Father knoweth that ye have need of all these things. But seek ye first the Kingdom (Consciousness) of God, and His righteousness (right ideas); and all these things will be added unto you." The kingdom of God is about right thinking, where you think only God's thoughts. I began to live in the light, light meaning living in God's holy thoughts. The light is also known as the Holy Spirit. By consciously asking in this way the energy of light the Holy Spirit is creating, transforming and assisting in making the change.

It took a miracle of an experience with God for me to know that God loves me and lives inside of me in the most incredible sacredness I could have ever known. The night before my surgery I was sitting up in my bed at home. I closed my eyes and began to pray for the healing of my body. As I prayed, I envisioned the doctor and the procedure that was to take place in the highest thoughts of God's loving care. Within a few seconds while I was still awake I felt my self being lifted above my bed into a beautiful golden light. This radiant light completely engulfed me. I felt surrounded in total loving of the Holy Spirit. The next day after the surgery the doctors told me there wasn't any cancer in the biopsy. The Holy Spirit had healed me. After a few days I went home and began a new journey of discovering myself and learning how to live in a greater way in God's holy thoughts.

I had to let go of my need for control by letting go of my addiction to fear. There was a purpose to my illness. The lesson for me was to love and accept myself as I am. To take care of myself *first*, so I could take care of others. The huge boulder on my back called fear and worry had to go. I had to re-evaluate what was important in my life from an intention of exploring a new way of living through *discovery*.

Learning through Discovery

One day long ago God wanted some ideas of where He could be placed where no one could see Him and only the wisest could find Him. He went to three wise men. The first wise man said, "Go to the highest mountain on earth surely only those who were the most devoted would make the trip to find you there." The second wise man said, "Go the bottom of the deepest sea, they would never find you there." God said, "No, someday there will be people able to climb the highest mountains and too they will have the ability to go to the deepest oceans. The third wise man said, "Put your self in the deepest part of everyone, go into the heart of each person, because no one would think to go inside to find God". God said that is the perfect solution.

Over a lifetime people have millions of experiences, yet how many learn the lessons? The attainment of wisdom has been slow and painful. Resistance to change and growth is considerable. It would seem that most people would rather die than alter their belief system. Living in the mind and emotions, trying to control the world, our spouses, children, bosses and friends makes life really hard. Trying to control our body and emotions is even more frustrating. Instead of living "out there" in the future trying to control the outcome of every situation and event, we have to embrace and direct our inner environment.

Right now I want you to begin to see your life as a classroom. Each day there are life lessons to learn and grow. In this classroom no one has to be perfect, just human. No matter what you have done, what mistakes you have made, what errors you have committed, you're not a failure until you lay down and quit. Whatever befalls us there is a blessing. Sometimes the blessing is in disguise, but it is a blessing nevertheless. This is because the fundamental nature of this world is to evolve toward a more harmonious and beneficial level of experience.

When life becomes a classroom, the manual you read comes through the wisdom of the heart and intuitive knowing. Come with me and *discover,* new techniques and ways to explore who you are through your inner creativity, an inner spiritual process where you will draw upon God and the Holy Spirit within, through "inspiration". It is a rich, exciting inner journey where you can learn how to heal past experiences of broken heartedness, mistakes, errors and failures. Learn how to feel worthy, safe and develop greater self-esteem.

First Key
Awareness

During the course of any normal day we think, say and do many things. The words we say and their intent have the greatest influence on how we direct our lives. In our fast paced society we ignore or forget how powerful words can be. Words evoke emotions, trigger memories and generate visceral reactions. Learning how to direct the mind and emotions is the difference of turning the darkness into the light. Your attitude plays back information and needs to be checked over regularly.

Emotions = energy in motion. People who live their lives allowing their mind and emotions to run their lives are like ships on the ocean without a mast or a rudder. They are subject to the prevailing winds (thought) and water (emotion) of the moment. These people are outwardly seeking happiness and excitement by going from one person or idea to another where their moods swing from feeling really high to the great depths of depression. Trying to please everyone, with no direction and no way of knowing what is real they put out false images of what people want them to be. With no boundaries to define themselves nothing is ever enough. They often walk away feeling lonely, rejected and misunderstood.

Feelings signal our state of being. Feelings tell us how we are doing, what matters to us, what needs changing, what is going well, and what is going badly. We are responsible for our own feelings. To disown our feelings and ignore responsibility for them is one of the most destructive things we can do both to others and to ourselves. When we take responsibility for our own disappointments, we are setting clear boundaries.

Think of driving your car. When you turn on the key, the energy of the car is started. When you put the car in gear, your car is ready to be directed into motion. Our body is much like a car. You think of something and then your emotions come into match the thought. When your emotions are in gear from reacting from fear or anger in a situation you can really get carried away, the next thing you know you're an accident waiting to happen. Awareness can be seeing your emotions from a place of "out of gear". Just neutrally observing how you feel about a situation before you put your emotions into gear. Slow down, instead of going 90 miles an hour with your mind and emotions, try 35 miles an hour for a while. Instead of reacting to a situation through fear, stop and take a deep breath and think about the situation and see if you can come up with at least three different ways to respond before speaking. This way you are embracing your inner thoughts and feelings by using discernment and wisdom. Ask yourself, "How will I feel about the outcome of this situation in a week or two?"

What are boundaries?

What would happen if you were driving down the interstate highway and there are no white lines on the highway, you can drive at any speed and in any direction? What a wild chaotic mess! With time as their enemy, that is how some people live their lives. A person who lives their life without priorities or boundaries is constantly running from one emergency to another, out of control while using everyone and everything in their obsessive game of power and control. Until one day they have a heart attack, car accident, loose their job or worse their life.

When we think of boundaries we think of limits. Boundaries give us a sense of what is part of us and what is not part of us, what we will allow and what we won't, what we will choose to do and what we choose not to do. My boundaries look like ten acres of land I call my Garden of Eden. My Garden is protected by an invisible energy field called an aura. [1ε] An aura is an invisible atmosphere supposedly surrounding a person or thing. We all have this energy field around us. Remember being in an elevator and feeling the person next to you, but you really didn't touch them? That is what I call my "ten acres" of energy; it is an aura of invisible light. It is important to honor your own personal ten acres and care for it.

[1ε] As defined in "The Auric Mirror" by Ella Vivian Power.

Our attitudes are our opinions about something. We are responsible for our own attitudes, for they exist inside our "property line", our Garden of Eden. They are within our hearts, not someone else's. God tells us to examine and take responsibility for the attitudes and beliefs that govern our lives. They form the structure of our personality. In the beginning of life, we "soak up" attitudes; as we mature, we need to take responsibility for making sure our opinions are ours and not someone else's. We choose them.

Honoring our self and honoring other people as separate from us is also an aspect of boundaries. Separateness is an important aspect of human identity. We are to be connected to others without losing our identity and individuality. We are to master the art of "being me without losing you." Without boundaries people are needy and demand a lot of attention. When there are unclear boundaries in any relationship, anger and resentment occurs as each person projects their unfulfilled need to be taken care of onto the other person. Developing our separateness involves knowing what our boundaries are. Knowing these boundaries helps us develop our separate and unique personalities.

"Treat others the same way you want them to treat you" Luke 6:31

Be courteous and have good manners. Always treat a human being as a person, that is, as an end in himself, and not merely as a means to an end. Strive to impart dignity and self-worth to all you meet. Your character is shown in many ways, but one of the most obvious is the way you treat people. You will grow in character and reputation if you treat others with kindness.

Try This Exercise

Create Your Garden of Eden

Imagine that you are standing on your own ten acres of land; it is your Garden of Eden. What does it look like? Where is it? Are there flowers and wildlife? Is there a house or dwelling? Who would you like to invite into your Garden of Eden? Write as much about your Garden as you can.

Try this Exercise in Priorities

Lets take some time and honestly look at your priorities. Listed below are 10 activities. Rank them in the order of their importance in your life. With 1 being the most important and 10 the least important. If there are any additional activities not listed write them in.

Play
Work
School
Friends
Children
God/prayer
Food/Nutrition
Community Service
Spouse
Rest/Sleep

A Dream Is a Wish The Heart Makes

I believe in the Golden Rule, which means to love God with all your body, mind and soul and your neighbor as yourself. That means to me that I must love myself and take care of myself *first* before I can really take care of others. My priorities look like this:

God/Prayer
Food/Nutrition
Sleep/Rest
Spouse
Children
Work
Play
Friends
Community Service
School

Now, compare your list of priorities and lifestyle to the one shown above. How are they different? How are they similar?

While its fine to put other things before God, you may not experience the oneness you are thirsting to have.

Grace Allison

Try this exercise in discovery

Has there ever been a time when you experienced broken heartedness? A time when you felt crushed inside by a loss of a loved one or someone has hurt you deeply or there was an injustice or circumstance that left you wounded? Take some time and write down the situation. What lesson did you learn from the experience? What blessing came out of the situation?

Chapter 7

The Value of Prayer

It takes practice to become more at-one, more honest more in tune with your self. To begin a life of living more with God and His loving there are three basic principles: discipline, devotion and introspection.

Our personality requires discipline for self control otherwise our physical desires, the unquenchable thirst for food, sex, love and other worldly objects gets out of control as we try to possess and control things and people. Making a commitment at an appointed time everyday to go inside and make contact with God through prayer and introspection builds confidence, detachment from worldly objects, inner strength, and compassion enabling us to give of our self to the world.

Devotion is love. We need devotion to establish a way of life in which we let go of the physical world and walk in the presence of God, reminding us of the first commandment requiring us to love God with all our heart, all our soul, and all our mind. Sometimes I think we give as much of our heart, soul and mind as possible to our fellow human beings, while trying hard not to forget God. We can at least say we are not forgetting God. But Jesus' claim is much more radical. He asks for a single-minded commitment to God and God alone. God wants all of our heart, all of our mind, and all of our soul. It is this unconditional and unreserved love for God that leads to the care for our neighbor, not as an activity, which distracts us from God or competes with our attention for God, but as an expression of our love for God who reveals Himself to us as the God of all people. When we go inside we are in devotion, a humbleness of the spirit appears, a connectedness to the Holy Spirit begins to take place. All of our anxieties, depressions and worries of the world are gone and replace with a tender loving.

Although I was raised in a very strict religious family, I did not know that God was loving and merciful. What I knew was to be afraid of Him, that I was a sinner beyond Him. And most of all that I was not worthy of His love. I was ignorant not a sinner I did not know any better. Like many people I was saying words to God with a feeling of being disconnected, that He was somewhere "out there", in the sky, in a minister, in a church … . but certainly not in *me*.

The need to feel validated leads me to fill my need for love and recognition in many areas outside of myself. My worth was validated with money and accomplishments I earned at work. Likewise, the more

I worked, the greater my false sense of self-esteem was rewarded. As I continued my life from a sense of lack and need I drew people and situations where I felt used and abused. Intimate personal relationships became a battleground of power and control. If I do this for you will you see me as a worthy person? Will you like me? Love me? Will you make me safe? Will you rescue me? Living in my mind, emotions and the low self-esteem of my false ego gave me great experiences and lessons.

Since my healing crisis in 1989, putting God first has made a world of difference in my life. Prayer has been a way-shower that helps me to stay centered in the gentle sweet happiness of my heart and wisdom of my mind and intuitive knowing. God and Jesus have become intimate personal friends. Each day when I pray and meditate I see them inside my creative imagination and I affirm each and every day that God loves me and gives me all good things. That I love Him and do only the things he would want me to do. Often I will share a situation or a person with Him and ask for a way I can know and understand how to handle a particular situation. In my mind and heart, God is everywhere and in everything. All things come from God and I give thanks for all I have and ask God to go forward to all people and situations in my life for the day and its events. I ask to be of service and surrender in loving trust to His loving care knowing He brings me all good things health, wealth, happiness, abundance, prosperity, riches through opportunities of loving, caring and sharing. With these blessings and intention I receive in loving gratitude all of His gifts allowing His Light to show me what is next for me to do.

God is not the bellhop in the sky to deliver every whim or wish. To let go and let God is to let go of false pride of "I Know" to one of surrendering the rationalizing (rationing lies) of your life to the truth of what is really going on. This takes great courage and maturity. Prayer is a personal encounter and a transforming one. Do not resist your negative thoughts and feelings, they will just continue to grow; instead embrace them by calling in God's loving light for the highest good and ask God to show you what to do and what the lesson might be that you are learning. Then let God know how grateful you are for His loving guidance and for all the gifts, talents, people and things you have in the material world. He truly does love everyone and is just waiting to pour out more of His abundance if only we would become a disciple through disciplining our self in daily prayer.

God does more than hear words He reads our hearts. Jesus taught that all good and bad originates in men's hearts. "A good man out of the good treasure of his heart bringeth forth that which is good; and an evil man out of the evil treasure of his heart bringeth forth that which is evil; for the abundance of the heart his mouth speaketh (Luke 6:45)

Although my audience for this book and manual is written predominately for Christians, I recognize and honor the different religious paths. As human beings in a sophisticated society, each culture

A Dream Is a Wish The Heart Makes

...s its own beliefs; each saying your way is different from my way, your ...vior is not my savior; your forever is not my forever. But the truth is, ...l life is one life. There is only one game in progress. This is one race, ...ith many different shades. We argue the name of God, what building, ...hat day, what ritual. What do his stories mean? Truth is truth. If you ...urt someone, you hurt yourself. If you help someone, you help ...ourself. Blood and bone are in all people. It's the heart and intent that ...atters. All life is everywhere.

...hatever religious belief you have follow it, whether it be Christian, ...uslim, Hindu, Hebrew, Jewish… there is truth and love in God's word ... every text and prayer. Make God and prayer first in your priorities of ...e and the boundaries you make will be easier and there will be more ...y, peace and happiness.

Try this God Bless You Exercise

Sit back comfortably in a chair, relax with your arms and legs uncrossed. Close your eyes and imagine that you are surrounded, filled and protected in God's loving light and as you see this, say to yourself" Father Mother God I ask just now that your Light surround, fill and protect. I want only to be able to see and hear that which is the truth and what is right for me now." Feel the warmth and security from within. Now that you are surrounded in love and truth take a deep breathe and say these words," God Bless You I love You". See these words going out then making an arc and coming back into your heart. Do this a few times. Breathe in this loving. You are now in touch with your own loving and God is filling your heart.

After doing this process for a few minutes just sit quietly and listen inwardly.

Open your eyes. Take a few deep breaths and write what you experienced.

Chapter 8

Image
I Am A God
Energized Be-ing

Imagine that each person born is innocent and naïve to the world. As we grow we learn the law of cause and effect that our attitude has a great deal to do with how we experience our life, "as a man thinketh in his heart he becomes" and as a result we develop a personality or self image.

The way I spell image – I Am A God Energized Being. We are spiritual beings having a human experience. We are made of God's Light and filled with God's loving energy. Our body is a sacred temple living in our own Garden of Eden where we are to be honored and cared for. Our mind and emotions are energy that fill our temple and Garden like a glass that is filled with Light or energy. If we have negative thoughts and feelings or any lack in self-esteem such as shame, guilt, apathy, grief, fear, lust or anger in our consciousness our temple in the Garden of Eden develops an energy leak. I call it "leaky consciousness". If there are a lot of feelings of unworthiness, then there are more energy leaks. These energy leaks separate us from the wisdom (Adam/mind) and love (Eve/heart). We get stuck either in the past holding onto a past hurt or in the future trying to control the outcome of events. Often to cover up or ease the pain of the energy leaks people will acquire addictions. These addictions are ways to temporarily feel good or happy. Food, alcohol, drugs, sex, work, worry and fear are all ways to mask our inner pain.

What do we really need to be a happy well-adjusted person? The basic needs for any one is food, shelter, air and love. Even having those things, most people still feel need or lack. You may covet many things, particularly material objects and experiences (a car, boat, a stereo, money, sex or maybe chocolate ice cream). Have you noticed when you first acquire or experience them that you may feel great and satisfied; but then, you distance yourself from that thing and go looking for something else to fill the lack or need? Have you ever gone to the grocery store when you were hungry? Did you buy things that you didn't really need because your hunger made those things look good? Ever go out to pick up a person when you were lonely or needy inside, or go shopping at the mall with your credit cards when you felt lonely or sad?

There is a difference in taking care of our basic needs and the need we feel from the deep lack of emotional fullness or emptiness.

The need to be rescued by someone or something outside of our self is responsible for co-dependant addictive and often abusive relationships, as well as financial and health problems. A constant need creates difficulty in all aspects of our life.

Whatever the goal in life keep your eye on the donut and not the hole.

Think how often we discipline our children with negatives. Don't fall. Don't touch that. Don't … Don't … Don't. Sometimes what may seem like disobeying could just be their unconscious processing the experience of falling or touching. Have you ever thought "I don't want to be in this job all my life", "I don't want to fail", "and I don't want to lose this sale"? Think about it. By the time your brain has got to the "don't" or "must not", your whole body has already received the message: fail, stay in the job, and miss the sale.

During my life changes I had to recognize that part of my driven life came from seeing my life from the hole in the donut. The training of my self was a challenge as I began to break old habits. I stand guard at the door of my mind and monitor my thoughts and what I want to create. In reflection I can see that negative thoughts were actually keeping me from having the thing I longed for, the more I desired the greater resistance. I was attracting to myself like a mirror only that which I was holding in my mind and emotions. Energy is everywhere in everything and God made everything so He is everywhere even in my negative thoughts. We cannot see radio or television waves yet we can see and hear the sound and images when they are received into these little boxes we have in our home. We cannot see the signals of our wireless telephones, yet we can talk to people anywhere in the world. The same is with our inner communication with God and the energy vibration and intention we transmit when we think and feel about something or someone. Have you ever thought of someone you haven't heard from for some time and then receive a telephone or letter the same day? We are all connected in God's loving threads of His Consciousness. It is tuning into the Light the Holy Spirit that is inside and creating a connection that you can feel and learn to trust.

God has given each person certain talents and abilities, and He holds us responsible for developing them. Many times people do not explore their own talents. They accept others definitions of who they are, without seeking if these definitions fit. We lose ourselves when we conform to others wishes for what we "should" be. We are separate people with separate identity. We must own what is our true self, and develop it with God's grace and truth.

How can we break the never-ending cycle of our broken heartedness, our leaky consciousness?

A Dream Is a Wish The Heart Makes

"Ask, and you will be given what you ask for, Seek, and you will find. Knock, and the door will be opened. For everyone who asks, receives. Anyone who seeks, finds. If only you will knock, the door will open." Matthew 7:7:8.

What is your dream? Are you a musician perhaps a singer who was told by someone that you have "no ear" and you can't sing? Music is not the only gift that can be lost or buried due to the power of negative words – sometimes an artist is not lost just badly wounded. Sometimes our parents have parental concern over our "heart breaks" of a creative profession. But how much more heartbreaking is it to have a parent who quelches your dream, refuses to acknowledge your gifts – even when they are seen or appreciated by others. The power of negative words can be just as abusive as if someone were to be physically hit. How many people have jobs they have resigned themselves to because of salereitus? Having a job for a salary is fine; it's when you are sacrificing yourself in a job for security that begins to diminish your spirit.

I know a doctor who I will call Phillip who practiced medicine for more than forty years who resented his work almost every day of his life. Phillip became a doctor because his father told him he was going to be a doctor. From the time Phillip could walk his father was trying to protect Phillip and guarantee his future by grooming him to become a physician. Doctors during the 1950's were well respected and financially secure. After medical school Phillip married a woman who later became his office manager. Over forty years until his wife died, they made a lot of money. However, due to his wife's health issues with cancer most of their life savings went to paying her medical bills. The financial security Phillip's father wanted for him was only temporary. What Phillip wanted was to be an artist, a painter and a writer; he refused to go against his father. It was too much of a risk to go for what he wanted. Phillip had rationalized that he didn't know how he was going to make money with his creative talents so he submitted to his fathers' wishes. When I met Phillip he was pursuing his dream of becoming an artist. He needed to be an artist so much that he took someone else's work by signing his name on some paintings and hung them in a local gallery. About a month later he got a call from the gallery, the real artist had come into the gallery and let the owner know *he* not Phillip was the real artist of the work. Phillip had rationalized how he was the artist by adding a few details and finishing the pictures. I felt sad for Phillip. I worked with him using the "A Dream Is A Wish That The Heart Makes" processes. After a few months Phillip enrolled in some art and writing classes. Recently I learned that he only works part time as a physician and is very happy pursuing his hobbies.

Choosing to be creative doesn't mean either/or. For example Phillip didn't realize what a gifted doctor and healer he was. During the forty years as a doctor he never considered doing anything artistic as a hobby because it was not income producing. When Phillip embraced his creativity for the enjoyment, he really became much happier and at peace both in his job as a physician and as a painter.

How many of us rationalize our lives? Perhaps not like Phillip where he became an imposter. However, we are imposters in our own way by pretending to be satisfied with our life when we are on the treadmill of no return. We rationalize our lives for all kinds of reasons. Rationalizing means to ration lies by telling our self something to white wash the truth. Being honest takes courage. Honest comes from the Greek, honest meaning to be at-one with your self, to be congruent.

When we feel honest and courageous we can see the fears of the unknown and yet also see possibilities of something new.

Try this Life
Dream exercise

If you were to be hon-est about your life what dream do you have in your heart that wants to be expressed?

Chapter 9

Keys of Awareness

We are creatures bound by physical needs, laws and limitations, yet we are also conscious co-creators of life who exude unlimited possibilities with every thought, movement, feeling and intent.

To change and direct ourselves takes a clear and strong intention. Like computers we are programmed to be who and what we are. Our mind is the hardware of the computer while the software or programs that our mind runs come from the experiences we have had during our lifetime. Years of programming from our family, friends, education, television, movies, music you name it, each and every moment we are being programmed by something. It often takes feeling disturbed with where were we are in our familiar place to overcome our resistance.

Grace Allison

A way to re-direct the darkness into the light is to bring the highest and fastest frequencies of the Holy Spirit into the lower and slower frequencies, in that way we are able to nullify and dissipate what we have come to know as our energy leaks. Like computers we are programmed to be who and what we are. With a strong intention and direction we increase the likelihood to change the inner programming. We overcome our resistance to our familiar thoughts and feelings of being out of control.

To create change we are going to be using a perspective that takes us out of [g]time, as we know it. I believe that we have time in the physical world so everything doesn't happen at once. However, in our mind, emotions and unconscious there is no time. Our mind and emotions can be thinking about something in the past at the same time we are experiencing something in the present. When I think of myself singing in the present, I can also be aware of an incident in my childhood where my parents said I was not good enough. With the feelings of rejection in that past memory I might not be able to sing with the depth of my heart. To heal the wound of the past we must go out of time, past the personality to the sacred part of us.

---

[g] Time as defined by Webster's Ninth New Collegiate Dictionary is, "the measured or measurable period during which an action, process, or condition exists or continues".

A Poem by Helen Mallicoat

I was regretting the past and fearing the future.

Suddenly, my Lord was speaking:

"My name is I AM," he paused.

I waited. He continued. "When you live in the past,

With its mistakes and regrets, it is hard. I am not there.

My name is not I was.

When you live in the future, with its problems and fear,

It is hard. I am not there. My name is not I will be.

When you live in the moment, it is not hard, I am here.

My name is I AM

Surely no word or phrase is less understood, nor more critical to comprehension of the Bible story, than **"I AM"**. And he said I am the God of your father, the God of Abraham, the God of Isaac, and the God of Jacob. Then Moses said to God, "If I come to the people of Israel and say to them, 'The God of your fathers has sent me to you,' and they ask me, 'what is his name? "Say this to the people of Israel (the) **'I AM** has sent me to you." And He also said to Moses, "Say this to the people of Israel, "The LORD, the God of your fathers, the God of Abraham, the God of Isaac, and the God of Jacob, has sent me to you' this is my name for ever, and thus (the) I am (is) to be remembered throughout all generations... ."

"Know thyself". This passage, "I AM THE I AM," can be understood only when it is seen that Moses stood at a critical point in human evolution when the Ego, mind, emotions and unconscious was making its transition from group or tribal soul to individual soul. Moses himself was gifted with the ancient and atavistic clairvoyance, and could not bring himself fully into the era of the developing "I AM"; hence he could not fully recognize it in the wilderness (Exodus 17,6; Numbers 20,11-12; Deuteronomy 32; 1 Corinthians 10,4)

When we say "I AM", we are in the present, our soul energy is being called forward and we are beginning to KNOW, who we are from the inner sacred part of us. Invoking this energy, can lift and change the inner consciousness, and experience the sacredness of who we truly are.

As we reawaken our creative imagination with introspection and discernment, the kingdom of heaven that is within can be experienced. Each person has the ability to tap in, utilize and direct it. Energy follows thought. As we become aware of how we are thinking, we can see how what we put out comes back. Then we can observe that what we focus on and put energy into is what we get. Through observation we can learn more about what we are doing and make a choice to change because we are creators.

In the next chapter you are going to fill the energy leaks in your temple and Garden of Eden by using the intention of "I AM". We are going to do a process based on neutral observation, trust and awareness. Change does not have to be hard or scary. Let us remember that every experience we have had or will have is one of learning. Little by little we will be removing judgments and elements of power and outward control. Right now, we are learning how to trust our self and the inner part of us that wants to heal and be whole. We are creating our own ten acres in our Garden of Eden from a sacred place of "I AM".

Chapter 10

Creating Your Dream

Like it or not life and living is about movement, advancement and change. People are nonliving when angry, depressed and feeling sorry for themselves or filled with fear. It's okay to try out negative emotions and how they feel but its not a place one would wisely want to stay. In the world as a classroom we get to see how it feels to be happy or sad, jealous or grateful, but you are supposed to learn from the experience and ultimately figure out which feels painful and which feels great. The healing of ourselves is to heal the wounded, diseased and injured where we have separated ourselves from the eternal being ness.

In this next exercise you are going to find where the fear, anger and depression are in your dream. Keep in mind the feelings and emotions are just energy leaks. We are going out of gear, observing our mind and emotions as we move through our inner resistance. In stating your dream, how do you feel? Be aware of the feelings attached to what you are asking for? There is a list of questions to ask your self to see where your resistance may be in what you are dreaming to have.

Create Your Dream Exercise

Step One

In reflection of your dream ask yourself the following questions to see where the resistance could be for you to have your dream. After each question, see if you feel any resistance; if you feel clear go to the next question.

1. Is it possible for someone to? Not just you, someone?

2. Is it possible for me to?

3. It is okay for me to?

4. Am I worthy to have or express this?

5. Is it safe for me to?

6. I deserve to?

7. I am permitted to?

8. I can?

9. I now am (doing) (having) (being)?

10. I am certain I am (doing) (having) (being)?

Step Two

Did you feel clear through the list of questions or was there one or more questions were you felt unclear? The inner feelings to have your dream could be very overwhelming at this point. That is okay. Just allow the experience to be. Which of the questions had the most resistance. Was it feeling safe or maybe it was feeling worthy? We are going to work with feeling safe or worthy.

Now take the negative feeling and make it into a positive statement. To heal the wound of the past we must embrace the negative, go past the personality to the sacred part of us, I AM. When we say, "I AM" we are in the present, our soul energy is being called forward and we are beginning to KNOW, who we are from the inner sacred part of us.

Write this statement:

I, **your name** AM now safe (or worthy) to have, (do or be) (my dream) of

(Fill in the blank).

At the end of the affirmative statement also include **easily, pleasurably, safely with fun, joy and enthusiasm for the Highest Good of All Concerned.** Remember our intent of how we direct our self is very important. We always use 'for the Highest Good of All Concerned' because if after going through the process of clearing and you still don't have what you want, it probably wasn't for the highest good. In some situations what you want could be coming in, just not in *your* time frame. Surrendering, letting go and letting God is important. For some people the dream may be opening you to receive something else that is even better and greater. The process of opening you to a sense of serendipity where you go out for one experience and find a better choice.

After you have written the affirmation then write all of the negative thoughts and feelings you may have that are in the way of you having your dream. Just let go, remember it is energy that needs to be released and let go.

Step Three

Have you written all of the negative thoughts and feelings to where you feel empty inside? Good, now take the negative thoughts and feelings you have written and either burn them (in a safe place like over the kitchen sink) or throw them away where you cannot see them again.

Next, you are going to fill the empty void with the God's loving. Just now find a comfortable chair to sit in. Relax with your arms and hand uncrossed. Then visualize in your mind the Light of God surrounding, filling and protecting you for the highest good and just ask, "Father Mother God I ask just now to be surrounded filled and protected by your most highest and loving light. Now ask for guidance in having your dream come true. Listen. Perhaps there are situations where forgiveness for yourself and others need to be done, if so just ask, 'Father Mother God I ask just now that I forgive myself in judging myself (in the situation, or with) <u>(fill in the blank)</u>. And I forgive <u>(the person in the situation)</u> for judging me.

Let go of any mental, or emotional baggage at this time. Give it up to God and the Holy Spirit inside of you. See yourself, your past situations and those you were involved with in perfect

Light and unconditional loving. When you feel complete, come back into your awareness in the room. Write down your experience.

Step Four

Now write:

1. Three things that you love:

2. Three things you are looking forward to:

3. Three things you are grateful for:

How do you feel now? Do you feel up lifted and connected inside where your heart, mind and emotions are all going into a positive direction? Great! You are on your way to having your dream or the one God wants for you.

Step Five

Continue to do this process, asking your self the questions listed in Step One where you experience the resistance to your dream each day for at least 30 days. It takes the practice of disciplining your self each day and your attitude toward your dream that determines whether or not you are successful.

After a week of doing the process of creating your dream, go back to the list of priorities on page eight and see if your priorities have changed. Also, take a look at your Garden of Eden. Have your boundaries changed? What does your Garden look and feel like now?

A Dream Is a Wish The Heart Makes

Success

By: Bessie Anderson Stanley (1904)

He has achieved success who has lived well, laughed often and loved much;

who has enjoyed the trust of pure women, the respect of intelligent men and

the love of little children; who has filled his niche and accomplished his task;

who has left the world better than he found it, whether by an improved poppy,

a perfect poem or a rescued soul;

who has never lacked appreciation of Earth's beauty or failed to express it;

who has always looked for the best in others and whose life was an inspiration;

whose memory a benediction.

www.ingramcontent.com/pod-product-compliance
Lightning Source LLC
Chambersburg PA
CBHW031427290426